I AM...

THIRTY NAMES GOD HAS GIVEN HIMSELF AND WHAT THEY MEAN

MICHELLE KEENER

Woodside Books

You may not know me, but I was thinking of you and praying for you as I wrote this book. As I scribbled notes on my legal pad, flipped through the stacks of commentaries and Bibles on my desk, and clicked away on my keyboard, you were on my mind.

I pray this book will be a blessing to you.

"The Lord bless you and keep you; the Lord make his face shine on you and be gracious to you; the Lord turn his face toward you and give you peace." (Numbers 6:24-26)

Soli Deo gloria

INTRODUCTION

One year ago, I was preparing for release of my first novel. In the build-up for the release, I wrote a devotional to give away to my website subscribers. It was called *You Are...Thirty Names God Has Given You and What They Mean*. It was meant to be a thank you gift to the people who were following, supporting, and encouraging me. I offered the ebook for free on my website and went back to preparing for the novel's release.

Then something strange happened. People started emailing me and reaching out on social media asking for paperback copies of You Are. I had a few copies printed and sent them off. Then more people asked, and more. Local churches started carrying it in their bookstores. My husband calls it "The Little Book That Could." *You Are...* took off in ways I had never anticipated, and it led me on an unexpected journey right up to this book you're holding in your hands.

I didn't start my writing career to write devotionals, but where God leads, we follow. There is incredible blessing in obedience to the call of God. His plan and His purpose are so much greater than we can imagine. Too often, we limit ourselves because we limit God. We think our dreams, our prayers, or our hopes are too big for Him. In our minds, we make God smaller than He is. We put imaginary limits on His power, His love, and His grace because we can't understand a limitless God. We make God like us and in doing so, we unknowingly put ourselves on His throne. We try to make God into something we can grasp, something our minds can rationalize.

But that is not God.

God is beyond our ability to understand. He is beyond our logical, rational explanations. God is God, and that is all we can say with absolute certainty. God is God, and we are not. That might sound like a poor place to begin a devotional about the attributes of God, but it is a necessary starting place. It is only in acknowledging our limitations that we can begin to rightly consider the limitlessness of God. When we bring a heart of humility to God He will reveal Himself to us more fully. God is beyond our biggest dreams and present in our smallest needs.

Any attempt to fully explain the majesty and wonder and power of God Almighty will fail, but it is still worth doing because it draws us closer to Him. We were created to be in relationship with God. As we study His attributes and the names He has given Himself in Scripture, we will begin to know Him more, and the more we know Him, the more we will trust Him. It's hard to trust someone you don't know. As a parent, I wouldn't leave my children in the care of a stranger. But someone I know, someone I am in relationship with, someone who has demonstrated faithfulness and love, that is a person I can trust with my children.

This is why we study God. We cannot know Him fully, but we can know Him. As we know Him more, our faith grows stronger. We trust His leading because we know He is trustworthy. We run to Him in our pain because we know He is faithful. We turn to Him in grief because we know He is our comfort. We rest in Him because we know He is our salvation.

Over the next thirty days, we're going to look at who God

says He is. It isn't a complete list, but it's a start. One day we will stand before Him in Heaven. We will worship at His throne and see Him face to face. His glory will surround us, and we will have eternity in His presence. Until that day, we can trust that His words are true and that He is who He says He is.

DAY ONE

GOD IS GOD

"I am that I am."
Exodus 3:14

*B*efore we can say that God is love, or that He is merciful, or that He is mighty, we must start with the simple truth that He is.

God is.

God exists.

His existence is the most basic and fundamental of His attributes, but it is one of the most complex for us to grasp. There is a God, and He knows your name. That realization should change everything about your life. We are not particles of matter that happened to come together in a grand cosmic accident. There is One who is bigger than our universe. He spoke a word, and galaxies burst into existence. At His command, stars began to shine, planets started to spin, and the sun ignited with fire and warmth. He said, "Let there be..." and the seas formed, mountains rose, and trees and flowers began to bud. He breathed life into the dust of the earth, and humankind was born.

God is the Author of existence because He has always existed. God has no beginning and no end. He is the Eternal One, the Ancient of Days, the Beginning and the End. No discussion of His attributes can begin unless we first settle the unshakable truth in our hearts that God is God, and there is no other. He alone is God. If we reserve any piece of the universe and dare to say that God is not in it, or that He did not create it, we negate everything. He is limitless, therefore we cannot limit His reach, His power, or His authority. There is no part of our life, our heart, or our world that is not God's. He is either God of everything, or He is not God.

In our ever-changing, always-shifting world, the truth of God's big-ness and His supremacy is something we can depend on. He is bigger than anything we will ever face. Whatever circumstances come against us, whatever trial or terror we endure, God is bigger. God is bigger than our darkest day and bigger than our greatest joy. There is nothing beyond His power and nothing beyond His reach. He is God. He cannot be overwhelmed, He cannot be caught by surprise, and He cannot be defeated.

God is eternal. He will never leave you. His presence will never cease. You can never run so far or fall so deep that God is not there, waiting for you. This God, this immense, immeasurable, limitless God, knows your name. He is the God of the universe and eternity, and He is also your God. He knows you, He sees you, and He loves you.

Prayer for Today

MIGHTY GOD,

I believe You are the God of all creation. You are the Undefeated One. You are always with me, and there is no place I can go that is out of Your sight. I praise You because You are God. You alone are worthy of worship and praise. The world in in Your hands, and You will never fail. Nothing I face is bigger than You or beyond Your control. Help me to remember that You are in control, You are with me, and You love me.

Amen

DAY TWO

GOD IS HOLY

"I am holy."
Leviticus 11:44

*H*oliness means set apart. God is holy because He is wholly apart. He is transcendent. There are only two categories in all of the universe and eternity when it comes to holiness: God, and everything that isn't God. God is sinless perfection. He doesn't meet a standard of holiness, He is the standard. God is holiness. Sin cannot exist in His presence. His holiness sets Him apart. In Revelation 4:8, we get a glimpse of the way Heaven worships God. "Holy, holy, holy is the Lord God Almighty, who was and is and is to come." The angles, elders, and every living creature in Heaven bow before His throne and worship Him because He is God Almighty. He is perfect in holiness, the only One worthy of praise.

As we love God, serve Him, draw close to Him, and learn of Him, we must not lose sight of His holiness and His majesty. The serpent in the Garden of Eden tempted Eve with the promise that she would be like God, but that desire to rise to His level, to somehow share in His glory, is a false promise. We will never be like God. His majesty has no end. His glory is endless and unmatched. We will never be able to understand Him fully, and we can never bring Him down to our level. God is beyond human imagination and beyond our grasp. Do we want a small god, something we can understand, analyze, and attain? No, because a god we can grasp is not a God who can save. The surpassing greatness of God reminds us that we are safe in His hands.

How do we deal with a God so holy, so majestic, and set apart that we cannot fathom His greatness? How can we even lift our eyes to such a glorious God? It is only by the blood of Jesus. Jesus makes us righteous. We can stand before God because we have been given the righteousness of Jesus Christ. We can approach the throne of God with boldness and confidence because we are His heirs. Nothing diminishes His glory, His might, and His holiness. We have been given access to His throne because we have been set apart by the blood of Jesus. We cry "Holy, holy, holy," because the cross made an eternity in His presence available to us.

Prayer for Today

HOLY LORD,

I worship You, God, in the splendor of Your holiness. I bow before Your throne and praise You with my whole heart. You are mighty and glorious, and I will never comprehend Your greatness. Thank you for making a way for me to be in Your presence. I come before You without fear because of Jesus Christ. You alone are God, and one day I will see You face-to-face and sing Your praises.

Amen

DAY THREE

GOD IS FORGIVING

"I, even I, am he who blots out your transgressions."
Isaiah 43:25

There's an old saying that says something sounds too good to be true, it probably is. It's a cliché that often holds true. That great deal might not be so great. That once in a lifetime opportunity might not be what we dreamed it would be. We have been scammed, lied to, and taken advantage of too many times. We are told to beware of things that sound too good to be true out of fear that we will be disappointed or ripped off.

For many, the Gospel sounds too good be true. Yet, every word of it true, complete, and available to each one of us. There are no strings attached, no bait and switch, no empty promises. The Gospel offers us the best deal in history. Jesus will take all of our sin and in return give us his righteousness. He will pay the debt we owe, and in exchange, he will give us his inheritance. All we have to do is say yes.

God has every right to keep a record of our wrongdoings. No matter what we do, however big or small, He is the One we sin against. We have broken His laws. We stand guilty before Him. He is the perfect judge; it is His right to decide the punishment for our transgressions. When confronted with our sins, what can we say? We have no defense.

But the story doesn't end there.

Jesus Christ, the Son of God, came to earth to be our defense. He bore our sin and shame. On the cross, he took our punishment. He paid our debt so we could be free. The cross is the Great Exchange. He took our sin and gave us his righteousness. We are no longer guilty before God. Our sins have not just been forgiven, they have been blotted out and erased from the ledger. They are gone forever. When God looks at you He doesn't see a record of wrongs that have been forgiven, He sees no wrongs at all. When He looks at you, He sees the righteousness of Jesus.

God is our Redeemer. He rescued us when we were lost and condemned. He redeemed us from the kingdom of sin and darkness and gave us a place in Heaven for eternity. The blood Jesus shed on the cross is the final payment for all of our sins. He paid the price for our salvation. Jesus made a way to reconcile us to God. He is the Lord who laid down his life for us. We didn't earn it. We didn't deserve it. It was a gift of grace from the God who loves us so much He didn't spare His own Son. When we accept that gift, we gain eternity in the presence of God.

Prayer for Today

DEAR LORD,

Thank you for the cross. Thank you for the gift of Your salvation. I admit that I need a Savior. I cannot save myself. I need You, Lord. Jesus,

I receive your salvation. You paid the price for my sins, and I surrender them all to you. I receive your righteousness and believe that I am redeemed. I am rescued. I belong to you, and my eternity is in your hands. Show me what it means to live for you. Fill me with your Holy Spirit and teach me to live for you.

Amen

DAY FOUR

GOD IS THE LORD

"I am the Lord and there is no other."
Isaiah 45:5

If God is God, do we really need to say that He is also Lord? Don't the two words mean the same thing? We often use the words interchangeably, but they mean different things. Look at what happened when Jesus appeared to the disciples after his resurrection. Thomas had been filled with doubt until Jesus appeared. When Thomas saw the scars in his hands and the wound in his side, he stopped doubting and believed. He exclaimed, "My Lord and my God!" (John 20:28). Thomas declared Jesus to be his God and his Lord.

God is God. Whether we believe it or not, whether we acknowledge His deity and His existence or not makes no difference. God is God, and nothing we do, say, or believe will change that fact. We do, however, have a choice in whether or not He is our Lord. When we accept Jesus as our Lord, we give him the right to be sovereign in our lives. He gets to lead us according to his perfect will. When we accept the Lordship of Jesus Christ, we lose nothing, and we gain everything. We gain his protection, his provision, his blessing, and most importantly his salvation. When Jesus is our Lord, we acknowledge his authority in our life. He gets to call the shots.

Sometimes we struggle with the idea of giving up control. We want to be the lord of our own life. We want to be in charge. It's my life so I know best, right? We may be willing to give God a little bit of control in certain areas. Maybe we decide to let God be Lord when we go to church, or if we're in a crisis we'll let God be in charge until the problem is resolved. But when it comes to our finances, our kids, or our career, we'd rather be in control and do things our way.

The problem with that way of thinking is that God is either Lord of every area of our life, or He is not Lord at all. We cannot pick and choose which areas we're willing to let God take the lead in and which areas we'll keep in our hands. To accept God as our Lord is to give Him full authority in every area of our life. If we try to delegate a little bit of lordship to God, while keeping some of it for ourselves, He isn't really our Lord. Whenever we try to tell God what to do, or where He can go, we will fail. God is not a second choice or a back-up plan. He must be our first choice, or He isn't a choice at all.

Prayer for Today

LORD GOD,

Today I acknowledge You as my Lord and my God. I cannot earn Your grace, and I cannot earn my way to Heaven. I accept the gift salvation that Jesus won on the cross. My past, my present, and my future are in Your hands. Lead, God, and I will follow. I give You every area of my life. I hold nothing back from You, Lord, because I know You love me, and You will not fail.

Amen

DAY FIVE

GOD IS UNIQUE

"I am God and there is none like me."
Isaiah 46:9

There is only one God. He is perfect, eternal, omniscient, and omnipotent. God alone is God, and nothing we imagine, build, or create can take His place. He is irreplaceable. And yet, so many people try every day to replace God. There is only one God, but there are far too many little gods we raise up in our lives every day.

We try to substitute something small and incomplete for the greatness of God. We put money and security before Him. We put our career and our success above Him. We put our family and our children ahead of Him. In thousands of tiny ways, we try to replace God, putting something else on His throne in our heart, turning to something else for our purpose, our protection, or our fulfillment. But God cannot be replaced. There is nothing in all of creation that comes close to Him. He alone is God, and there is nothing like Him.

Anytime we turn to something other than God, we are making tiny idols for ourselves. We may hear the word idolatry and think of the golden statue in the Book of Daniel or the household gods of the Canaanites, but idolatry can be much more subtle than that. Idolatry happens whenever we give something other than God the first place in our heart. Money can easily become an idol. Work and our career can be an idol. Even our good deeds can be an idol. Anything that takes the place of God in our life, no matter how admirable, noble, or good it sounds, is an idol.

God wants to be first in your life. That is His place. He alone is worthy of your worship, He alone is worthy of your praise. He alone is your salvation and your security. God is the only thing that can ever satisfy. He is the only thing that will never betray you, disappoint you, or fail you. Even the greatest and most worthy things in this world are passing and will eventually fade away. God alone is eternal and unchanging. We cannot meet the eternal longing in our heart with a temporary fix. We were created to worship, praise, and abide in the presence of God Almighty. Fix your gaze on Him, and you will find love and grace beyond your wildest imagining.

Prayer for Today

DEAR LORD,

You alone are God. There is none like You and nothing can replace You. I give You all of my worship and my praise. Forgive me for the times when I have put something else above You in my heart. Help me to fix my eyes on You and to always put You first. You alone are my God.

Amen

DAY SIX

GOD IS ABLE

"I am God Almighty."
Genesis 17:1

In Genesis 17, God appears to Abraham. It has been thirteen years since the Lord first told Abraham that he would have a son and that his descendants would be as numerous as the stars in the sky. All these years later, God appears and renews His covenant with Abraham and once again tells him that he will have a son and become a father of nations. Abraham is ninety-nine years old, and his wife Sarah is ninety. Surely the idea of having a baby at their age seemed impossible.

Yet, in the face of these impossible circumstances, God revealed something about Himself to Abraham. "I am God Almighty" (Genesis 17:1). The name God Almighty comes from the Hebrew word *El-Shaddai*. This name for God speaks of His power. It is no mistake that God uses it when He reminds Abraham of this seemingly impossible promise. There is nothing God cannot do. He is *El-Shaddai*, God Almighty. A year later,

Sarah gives birth to a son. Through his son Isaac, Abraham does indeed become the father of a great nation, the nation of Israel.

In His name, God Almighty, God reminds us that He is all-powerful, and He can do anything. His power has no end. God is always able. He can stop the sun in its path, He can rescue three men from a fiery furnace, and He turn an enemy army against itself. There is nothing too hard for God. When we are weak, He is strong. When we are struggling, He is the answer. When we feel lost, in Him we are found.

There is no power that can defeat Him, and no power that can limit Him. God can do all things because there is nothing in all eternity that can withstand His power. No matter what God does, His power is never diminished. He cannot be worn down. He cannot lose strength. What He gives, He does not lose. His power is unstoppable and unending.

God is the source of our strength. We have victory over sin and death because of what He has done. We walk in righteousness because of what He accomplished. In God we have all we will ever need. He is our provision and our protection. When we recognize Him as God Almighty, we can take comfort in knowing that we are on the side of the undefeated and the undefeatable. God is sovereign over everything. He is King of Kings and Lord of Lords. There is nothing that comes against us, no financial difficulty, no illness, no persecution, no anxiety, no mistake, no failure, no disappointment, that will shake Him. God is more powerful than any adversary we face. He is forever victorious, and when we cling to Him, we become victorious.

Prayer for Today

DEAR GOD,

You are God Almighty, the Sovereign One. There is nothing You cannot do. You are in control, and I trust You. When circumstances try to overwhelm me, when fear tugs at me, remind me that You are El-Shaddai, God Almighty. You are God over impossible situations. Your will is always good, and Your purpose will always prevail. Fill my heart with fresh trust and confidence in You and Your mighty power.

Amen

DAY SEVEN

GOD IS THE BEGINNING AND THE END

"I am the Alpha and Omega."
Revelation 22:13

Alpha is the first letter of the Greek alphabet and Omega is the last. By using those letters together, Jesus is not only saying that he is the beginning and the end of all things, but that he is also in the middle of all things. Just as when we say, "that covers everything from A to Z," Jesus is saying that he is present in everything from the beginning to the end. As Alpha and Omega, Jesus isn't just at the beginning and the end, he is present and active through all things.

Jesus is eternal. He is eternally coexistent with God and the Holy Spirit. There has never been a time when the Trinity was not whole, complete, and in perfect unity. From before God spoke creation into existence, Jesus was present. Jesus is the Alpha, the beginning of creation, because he was before creation, and he is the Omega because he will be at the end of creation.

Everything originates in God and ends in Him. No matter how big our universe gets, it is always held in the hands of God.

Think of a jigsaw puzzle. When we turn the box over and dump all the pieces onto a table, we have an entire puzzle to assemble. Shapes, colors, images, the pieces get pushed about on the table as we move them and shift them until they fit. Eventually a beautiful picture is formed. But that puzzle, for all of its pieces, was held by the table. From the beginning to the end and all throughout the process, the table was present. The puzzle may have looked like a finished project, but it was upheld by the table. A table that existed before the puzzle began and a table that was still there long after the puzzle had been put away. It's an imperfect metaphor, but it's a reminder that however much we strive with the puzzle pieces of our lives, God was there before we began, and He will be there long after our life on Earth is over. God is the Eternal One. He holds every piece of our life in His hands.

The eternity of God isn't easy to comprehend. He has no beginning and no end. When creation began, God was already at its end. He has seen the end from the beginning. God is the only One who can speak with absolute truth and authority because He has seen it all. His love is eternal; His plan extends beyond time. While we may struggle with a five-year plan for our life, God planned our redemption before the universe began. There is nothing God has not seen, no outcome that can surprise Him. When the pieces of our life don't make sense to us, when we aren't sure how they fit, God is there. He is holding all the pieces. He formed them and He knows exactly where they go. In His hands, our life becomes a masterpiece for His glory.

Prayer for Today

ETERNAL GOD,

You are the beginning and end. There is nothing beyond Your care. You formed me in my mother's womb, and You were with me at my first breath. You have walked with me every day of my life, and You will be with me when my life is over. When I open my eyes in eternity, I will see You face-to-face and worship in Your presence.

Amen

DAY EIGHT

GOD IS PERSONAL

"Don't be dismayed for I am your God."
Isaiah 41:10

God is God of the whole universe. He is the Author of life. He is the One who holds all of creation in His hands. He is the God who created the mountains, the stars, and the sun. He commands the winds and tames the seas. God is God over all.

He is also your God.

Yours.

God is not distant and far off, unapproachable and terrifying. He is beside you, walking with you through every minute of every day. He is the God who formed you in your mother's womb. He knew every day of your life before you took your first breath. God is your biggest fan and your strongest champion. He is your God.

In the book of Genesis, when Hagar is pregnant with Abraham's son, she flees to the desert where she encounters an angel of the Lord who comforts her and speaks a blessing over her. Hagar gives God this name, "You are the God who sees me" (Genesis 16:13). In the middle of the desert, God saw Hagar. He heard her cry and met her need. God sees you. He sees your need. God is not so big that He cannot see each individual person. He sees each one of His children, including you.

Years later, in the book of 1 Samuel, Hannah prays for a child. When God blesses her with a son, she sings a song of praise. Hannah says, "the Lord is a God who knows" (1 Samuel 2:3). God knows you. He knows every hair on your head. He knows your deepest hurts and your biggest dreams. God knows everything about you. There is nothing hidden from Him. The secrets in your heart, God knows them. The mistakes you've made, the pain you endured, God knows it all. Not one tear you've shed, not one wound you've suffered, not one moment of success has gone unnoticed. God knows you, and He loves you.

God is so huge, so incomprehensible, that we can spend a lifetime studying Him and still only scratch the surface of His immeasurable, unfathomable glory. But God is also intimate. He is close to you. He cares deeply about every detail of your life. God is God over the whole world, billions and billions of people, but He is also your God. He sees you, and He knows you. He has a plan and a purpose just for you. God is there to strengthen you when you're weak, help you when you're in need, and uphold you when you fall. God is by your side and on your side. He is your God.

Prayer for Today

FATHER GOD,

You are my God. You see me, and You know me. There is no place I can go where You will not be. You are always with me. You created the universe, and yet You know every hair on my head. When I feel alone, remind me that You are with me. When I feel overlooked, remind me that You have seen every second of my life. When I struggle, remind me that You are on my side.

Amen

"I am a God who is near and far away."
Jeremiah 23:23-24

The day my sixteen-year-old daughter got her driver's license, she asked to go to the store by herself. On the way home, she took a wrong turn and got lost. When she was late coming home, we knew something was wrong, but we didn't know what happened. My husband got in his truck and followed her GPS signal. Driving alone at night, my daughter was scared and lost and couldn't find her way home. When she finally pulled over, she looked in her rearview mirror, and through her tears she saw her Daddy's truck. It was when she stopped trying to figure it out on her own, when she stopped running, that she stopped being lost and became found.

Our God has never-failing GPS. We are never out of His sight. He is both near to us and far away. He is with us as we journey, and He is waiting for us at our destination. God is not bound by time or geography. He is every*where* and every*when*. Heaven and

Earth are full of His presence. We cannot hide from Him, and we cannot be lost by Him. When we stop running and turn our eyes to Him, we will see that He has always been there. If we focus on the wrong things, we may not see Him, but that doesn't mean He isn't there. God is with you, right now, this second; the only question is whether you are looking at Him or looking at your circumstances.

Nothing can separate us from God. The Apostle Paul explains it clearly, "neither death nor life, neither angels nor demons, neither the present nor the future, nor any powers, neither height nor depth, nor anything else in all creation, will be able to separate us from the love of God that is in Christ Jesus our Lord" (Romans 8:38-39). Not even our own distraction, bitterness, or foolish choices can separate us from God. You are never hidden from Him, and you are never beyond His reach. God will never leave you. He is always with you, and He is always waiting for you. There is no place you can go that God has not already been. There is no place He is leading you that He has not already prepared for you. When you feel lost and alone, stop and turn your eyes to God. You will see that He was always there.

Prayer for Today

Mighty God,

Thank You, Lord, for being with me. I am never alone because You are always beside me. I am never lost because You know right where I am. You have prepared a place for me, and You are leading me. When circumstances are scary, when I get distracted, help me keep my eyes on You. Remind me, God, that Your presence fills the whole earth, and I am never beyond Your reach.

Amen

GOD IS IN CONTROL

"Be still and know that I am God."
Psalm 46:10

It doesn't matter what is going on around us, God is still God. He is our point of certainty. He is the unchanging, unsurprised, fixed center of eternity. Nothing can shake Him, nothing can defeat Him. When circumstances fill us with anxiety, when we worry, when fear rises within us, we can take comfort in knowing that God is still God. There is nothing beyond His control. Nation may rise against nation, but God is King over them all. Every nation on earth, every moment in history is under His sovereign control.

That can be hard to remember when we're facing something scary. When we get a medical diagnosis, when we suffer financial loss, when we lose a loved one, when a marriage crumbles, it can feel like the world is falling apart. But God has not failed. Circumstances may feel out of control, but we can be still and know that He is God. Being still before God is stepping back and allowing Him to take the lead. When we know that God is in charge, we can stop trying to control everything ourselves. And doesn't that sound wonderful? We don't need to have all the answers, we just need to know the One who does.

When we lay aside our agenda, surrender to God, and follow His leading, things change. In His hand broken marriages can be restored, shattered dreams are rebuilt, and hopeless situations become testimonies of His goodness and grace. No matter what we face, when we are still before God, resting in His presence, and trusting in His sovereignty, we are acknowledging that He is God and we are not.

There will come a day when God is exalted before all nations and all people. At the name of Jesus every knee will bow and every tongue confess that he is Lord. We don't have to wait for that day. We can do that today. We can exalt God and proclaim Him to be Lord right now, this minute. We can be still and rest, knowing that He is God.

Prayer for Today

MIGHTY GOD,

Thank you, Lord, that You are God over all. Nothing is beyond Your control. You are never shaken and never overwhelmed. I surrender every situation into Your hands. I trust You because Your will is always for my good. Have Your way in my life. Lead me in the direction of Your sending, and I will follow. Have Your will in every circumstance I face.

Amen

"When they cry out to me, I will hear, for I am compassionate."
Exodus 22:27

Compassionate, merciful, gracious. God is unfailing in His love for His people. It is His nature to show compassion, extend mercy, and be gracious to His children. It is not just something God does, it is who He is. When we feel compassion, it's an emotion that may come and go. Compassion is an emotion we feel, it isn't who we are. Not with God. God's mercy isn't a fleeting impulse, it is a part of His character. His mercy is never-ending. His compassion never runs dry. His grace is unlimited.

The Hebrew word used in this verse is *channun* and it means gracious. To be gracious is to show kindness, favor, or compassion, to show mercy. Even when we don't deserve it, even when we fall and fail, God shows us favor and compassion. When we deserve punishment, God gives us mercy. Nowhere is this seen more clearly than on the cross. Jesus took on the punishment we deserved and gave us his righteousness instead. Out of His love for us, God shows us mercy and grace.

Grace is God's unmerited favor. Unmerited means we do not deserve it, and we cannot earn it. We cannot take any credit for it because it is solely dependent on God and what He has done. If grace was something we could earn or buy, it wouldn't be grace. Grace is a gift from a compassionate Father to His children. God made a way for all of us, every single person on earth, to live in forgiveness and freedom.

In the New Testament, Jesus was moved by compassion many times.

"When he [Jesus] saw the crowds, he had compassion on them, because they were harassed and helpless, like sheep without a shepherd" (Matthew 9:6).

"Moved with compassion, Jesus touched their eyes; and immediately they regained their sight and followed Him" (Matthew 20:34).

"When He went ashore, He saw a large crowd, and felt compassion for them and healed their sick" (Matthew 14:14).

Miracles follow God's mercy. When we cry to Him, He hears and responds. God heard the cries of His people in Egypt, and He sent Moses to deliver them. God saw His children in bondage to sin, and He sent His Son to save us. It is His compassion that breaks chains. It is His grace that sets us free. We have nothing to offer and nothing to bribe Him with. We cannot buy or earn His grace. It is a free gift from God because of His great love for us.

Prayer for Today

MERCIFUL GOD,

Thank you for Your grace. You have given me so much, and because of Jesus You don't hold my mistakes against me. In Your great mercy

You have given me eternity in Your presence. You have filled me with Your love. Your mercy is new every morning and it never runs out. When my heart is heavy, I will turn to You. Let Your compassion wash over me and restore me.

Amen

DAY TWELVE

GOD IS WILLING

"I am willing."
Matthew 8:3

There is a passage in the Gospel of Matthew that speaks to the great willingness of God to bless His people. "A man with leprosy came and knelt before him and said, 'Lord, if you are willing, you can make me clean.' Jesus reached out his hand and touched the man. 'I am willing,' he said. 'Be clean!' Immediately he was cleansed of his leprosy" (Matthew 8:2-3) .This man came to Jesus with a disease that made him an outcast. He was unclean. He wasn't welcome in the temple. He was sick, alone, and in desperate need. He knelt before Jesus and said, "*if you are willing*." He didn't doubt Jesus's power to heal him, he doubted his willingness.

I have done that many times myself. I know God can work in my life, I know is He is able to move in a miraculous way, but sometimes I doubt He will. How often do we bring a heart of doubt to God? We know He is capable, but we worry that He is unwilling. Why would God help me, we ask. Why would God do this for me? A voice in our head whispers, I don't deserve it. I haven't earned it. How many times have we talked ourselves out of a blessing simply because we were so sure God was unwilling that we refused to even ask?

The leper came to Jesus, laid his pain at his feet, and Jesus met him right where he was. He didn't ask for obedience, he didn't ask for great works, he heard the man's cry and he responded, "I am willing." Jesus was willing to touch a man society had labeled unclean. He was willing to heal, save, and restore.

He still is.

God is not far off. He is with us in our pain. Jesus touched the leper because he was with him, close enough to reach out his hand and touch the sores on his skin. God is not removed from the suffering of life. He is not distant and unreachable. When we come to God, He meets us where we are. He is with us in our joy and our sorrow. He is with us in our triumph and our despair. When we cry to God, He hears us, and He is willing. He is willing to strengthen us, heal us, sustain us, and bless us.

Doubt tries to steal what God has said, but His Word is true. He loves you, He hears you, and He is willing.

Prayer for Today

FATHER GOD,

I believe that You are willing. Your heart towards me is filled with love. You hear my every prayer, and You are willing to bless me. You are willing to heal me. You have withheld nothing from me, even sending Jesus to die on a cross to save me. Forgive my times of doubt and remind me that Your love is never-ending, and Your plan for me is good. I lay my needs at Your feet and trust that You are willing.

Amen

GOD IS YOUR HEALER

"I am the Lord who heals you."
Exodus 15:26

I remember being a young child and falling down the steep driveway in front of my house. I scraped my knees and hands pretty badly. I burst into tears and immediately ran to my dad. He cleaned my wounds, put on bandages, and held me as I cried. I was hurt, so I went to my father.

Our Heavenly Father wants us to run to Him when we are hurting. In His arms we will find healing, rest, comfort, and restoration. Whatever wounds we suffer, whatever pain we endure, whatever hurt we face, God can heal them all. In Exodus 15:26, God reveals Himself to be *Yahweh-Rapha*, The Lord who Heals. It is part of who He is. God is the only One who can bring us true and lasting healing from our deepest wounds.

In the New Testament, a woman who had been afflicted with bleeding for twelve years came to Jesus. She grasped the hem of his garment, and she was immediately healed. After years of suffering, she brought her pain to Jesus, and she was healed. Jesus did not reject her. When society ostracized her and turned her away, Jesus brought her close and healed her. The secret pain we endure, the disappointments and rejection, the wounds of our past, all of the yucky, embarrassing things we try so hard to hide from others, are the very things God wants to heal in our lives. God will not turn away from you. There is nothing in your past that will make God stop loving you, and there is nothing He cannot heal.

Every healing we will ever need was accomplished two thousand years ago on the cross. Jesus bore all of our brokenness in his body. Isaiah 53:5 says, "by his wounds we are healed." It is through the wounds Jesus suffered that our wounds are healed. He was raised to life again, his body healed and restored, and it is through him that we are healed and restored.

Yahweh-Rapha is our healer. He takes the broken pieces of our lives and makes them into something beautiful. God brings hope where there was despair. He brings peace where there was torment. He brings life where there was death. Whatever we bring to God and lay in His hands, He uses for good. We may not always understand what He's doing, but we can trust that He is at work, and He will not fail.

Prayer for Today

FATHER GOD,

You are my healer. I lay all of my hurt, all of my pain, all of my wounds at the foot of the cross. Your word says that it is "by his wounds we are healed." It is because of Jesus and his shed blood, that I am healed. I trust in Your love and Your power. You are Yahweh-Rapha, the Lord who Heals, and there is nothing beyond Your reach.

Amen

DAY FOURTEEN

GOD IS YOUR COMFORTER

"I am the one who comforts you."
Isaiah 51:12

Have you ever cried so hard you couldn't breathe? When your heart was broken, and the pain was so overwhelming that you couldn't even speak? Have you experienced a hurt so deep you thought it would never end? I have experienced intense, blinding, physical pain I thought I couldn't endure, and I've had my heart so shattered I thought it would never mend. Suffering has a way of stripping away all of our defenses, leaving us raw and exposed. When we suffer, we need comfort. We don't need empty words or flimsy attempts to cheer us up. We need someone to sit with us in our pain and bring us comfort that binds the wounds of our hearts and whispers words of love. That someone is God.

God is your comforter.

God is the only One who understands the depth of our pain. Five years ago, I suffered a terrible burn on my leg. It was ugly and brutal, and it was the worst pain I have ever felt. I tried to describe the pain to my family, but no amount of words was enough. None of them could understand the constant agony of that burn. But God did. I didn't need to explain it to God. I didn't need to describe it or tell Him why or how it happened. He already knew. He met me in my pain, wrapped me in His arms, and carried me through it. He didn't stop the pain, but He bore it with me.

God meets us in our pain. He comes to us in our greatest need and sits with us. He is the Comforter who never leaves. He wraps His arms around us and holds us close. Our pain doesn't drive Him away, it doesn't scare Him, and it is never too much for Him. God is the One who soothes our wounds. He is the One who envelopes us in His love and speaks words of love over us.

The Apostle Paul writes that He is "the God of all comfort, who comforts us in all our troubles" (2 Corinthians 1:3-4). There is nothing we experience that is beyond His comfort. In every situation, in every broken part of our life, in every pain, every betrayal, every disappointment or failure, God is our comfort. There is no trouble we face, no hurt we endure that God cannot meet. It is only when we suffer that we experience God as Comforter. When things are going well, when we're satisfied and healthy, when life is safe and secure, we may experience God in other ways. However, it is only in suffering that we experience His immense, unending, all-encompassing comfort. God meets us in our pain and reveals Himself to us as our Comforter. When hurt comes, and it will because we live in a fallen world, we can turn to God, and in His arms, we will experience His precious comfort.

Prayer for Today

DEAR LORD,

When I am in pain, I will turn to You. You are my Comforter. I surrender my hurt to You. I give You my disappointments, my regrets, and my suffering. I cling to You and receive Your comfort. You are not afraid of my pain so I lay it all at Your feet. Show me Your comfort Lord, surround me with Your love and strengthen me when I feel weak. You are my God and I run to You.

Amen

DAY FIFTEEN

GOD IS WITH YOU

"Do not be afraid, for I am with you."
Genesis 26:24

Our society is more connected than ever before. We have cell phones, email, text messaging, and social media. We are never more than a wi-fi connection away from billions of other people. Yet, many of us have never felt more alone. Screens have often replaced relationships, and when storms hit, when our lives are tuned upside down, we may find ourselves alone and scared.

But we are never alone.

God has promised that He will always be with us. No matter where we go, God is already there. God is with us in every step of the journey. There has never been a time when we were left on our own. God will never abandon us. He will never leave us. In the fiercest storm, God is there. This promise is repeated time and again in the Bible. When Joshua was preparing to lead the

Israelites into the Promised Land, knowing they would face war, God told him, "Do not be afraid, for I am with you" (Genesis 26:24). Joshua and the Israelites would not have to face their enemies alone. God tells Joshua not to fear because He was with him. It is God's presence that banishes fear.

Remember when you were a small child. The world was a big, scary place, but when you reached for the hand of your mother or father, fear disappeared. Why? Because their presence was all you needed to feel safe, protected, and cared for.

In God's presence there is security. In His presence there is safety. The storm may rage around us, financial difficulties may try to overwhelm us, relationships may break our heart, but God is with us. When we remember His presence, we overcome fear. It's never about us, how strong we are, or what we can do, it's all about the One who is with us. We are with the One who has overcome the world. We are with the One who holds the universe in His hands. God is with you. His presence and His love are your shield and your fortress. God is on your side. He is in your corner. He will never leave you or forsake you. He has chosen you and called you His own.

In the Gospel of Matthew, Jesus reminds his disciples of this precious promise. "And surely I am with you always, to the very end of the age" (Matthew 28:20). God is with you always. When fear rises in your throat, when anxiety fills your heart, close your eyes and remember that you are not alone. God is with you always, even to the end of the age.

Prayer for Today

FATHER GOD,

Thank you for Your presence. Thank you for being with me, now and always. Remind me that I am not alone. You have promised to be with me, and You always keep Your promises. When I am afraid, I will trust in You. Every step I take You are with me. Thank you for never leaving me, thank you for walking with me through all my ups and downs. You are with me, so I will not fear.

Amen

DAY SIXTEEN

GOD IS LIGHT

"I am the light of the world."
John 8:12

Have you ever walked into a dark room? Did you walk carefully, trying not to bump into things or stub your toe while you tried to find the light switch? Maybe you didn't know which way to go, or where things were. You couldn't see obstacles in your path or potential dangers lurking in the shadows, but when you flipped on the light, the darkness vanished and everything became clear.

Jesus is our light. We were in darkness, lost in a world of sin and shadows. We couldn't see the path before us or the danger that lay ahead. Jesus pierced the darkness and led us into the light of his presence. Jesus enables us to see the world rightly. He is the light that dispels the darkness of sin, doubt, and fear.

When you were a child the night probably seemed scary. Shadows might be monsters. Dark corners might be hiding something terrifying. Once the light came on and you saw things clearly, the fear fled. Even now, as adults, how many of us lay awake at night and listen to worry and anxiety that whisper through the darkness? It is the light of Jesus that silences those fears. His light triumphs over darkness.

The world around us tries to offer all kinds of counterfeit light. Advertisers tell us we need to buy more things, have a bigger house, or buy a better car. The world says we need to be famous, get a promotion, or make more money to be important. Social media says we need more likes and shares to have influence. All of those paths may be lit up with flashing neon lights, but they end in darkness. Only Jesus is the light that will never fail. "When Jesus spoke again to the people, he said, 'I am the light of the world. Whoever follows me will never walk in darkness, but will have the light of life" (John 8:12).

Light banishes darkness, but darkness cannot banish light. It is a one-way street. A single match can defeat an entire room of darkness. When light is present, darkness must flee. When we follow Jesus, we walk in his light, and the darkness cannot come near. In Jesus, we see rightly. The lies of the dark are revealed, and the dangers that were hidden are seen. He is the light of the entire world, a light that is available to everyone, and no darkness can stand against him.

Prayer for Today

DEAR GOD,

You are the light that I follow. Help me to see rightly. You pierced the darkness of my life and showed me Your marvelous light. Help me to follow You and walk every day in the light of Your presence. Where You go, darkness must flee. I cling to You, my light and my salvation.

Amen

GOD IS THE GOOD SHEPHERD

"I am the good shepherd."
John 10:11

We are the sheep, and God Himself is our Shepherd. A shepherd guards and guides his sheep. It is the shepherd who leads them in and leads them out. He directs them to good food and clean water. It is the shepherd who cares for them, sheers them, and protects them. Jesus is the shepherd of his flock, all those who follow him and are called by his name belong to him. He is our guide and our protector.

Not only does Jesus declare that he is the Good Shepherd, he explains what makes a good shepherd. "I am the good shepherd. The good shepherd lays down his life for the sheep" (John 10:11). A good shepherd is prepared to defend his sheep to the death. A good shepherd will fight off wild animals and thieves to protect the sheep that belong to him. Jesus not only said it, he did it. Jesus is the Good Shepherd who fought to the death for his sheep. He defended us all the way to the cross. Our Good Shepherd laid down his life for us. He stood between us and death. He placed himself between us and all the forces of hell. He bore the punishment of sin so that it would not fall on us. He is the Good Shepherd who sacrificed his life for the sheep he cares for.

A good shepherd is not the same as a hired hand. "The hired hand is not the shepherd and does not own the sheep. The sheep do not belong to him So, when he sees the wolf coming, he abandons the sheep and runs away" (John 10:11-12). The hired hand abandons the sheep when danger comes. The hired hand cares more for his own life than he cares for the sheep. When terror threatens, when bad news comes, when difficulties arise, the hired hand would rather run away than stay and fight. When we place our trust in anyone other than Jesus Christ, we are at the mercy of a hired hand that cannot save when danger comes.

Jesus is the Good Shepherd because he knows who belongs to him. "I am the good shepherd. I know my sheep and my sheep know me" (John 10:14). We belong to him. We are the sheep in his care. When we know our shepherd, we will follow his voice, trusting in his leading. Sheep who know the voice of their shepherd will not follow another. We are safe in his care because he is the Good Shepherd who laid down his life for his sheep.

Prayer for Today

Dear Lord,

You are the Good Shepherd. You have led me into a good land, and Your hand is with me. You are my protection and my guide. You know my name. When I am lost, You come and find me. When I am in danger, You are my Defender. You laid down Your life for me and saved me. Help me to hear Your voice and follow after You.

Amen

"I am the bread of life."
John 6:35

Just as our body needs food to survive, our spirit needs God. Without food, our body will die, and without God, our spirit will wither. Jesus is our spiritual food. It is from his presence that we gain strength. When we feed ourselves the Word of God, when we spend time with Him, drawing ever closer to Him, we grow stronger. My dad used to tell me I had to eat my vegetables to grow big and strong. We need to feast on the Word of God for our spirits to thrive.

Jesus fed thousands with two fish and a few loaves of bread. He satisfied their physical hunger, and then told them he was the true bread they needed. Jesus stood before a crowd that had eaten their fill of earthly food and said, "I am the bread of life. Whoever comes to me will never go hungry, and whoever believes in me will never be thirsty" (John 6:35). Even after the biggest Thanksgiving feast, we will all be hungry again. Not even three servings of turkey and pumpkin pie will satisfy us forever, but Jesus is the bread that will satisfy our spiritual hunger. When we believe in him, we will never be hungry because our spirit will have been fed for eternity.

So many people today are searching for something to fill the ache in their souls. They go from one workshop to another, trying one religion after another, searching self-help books and listening to motivational speakers to fill the emptiness inside. It is all temporary food, a quick meal that will leave their spirits hungry again. Only Jesus can satisfy every longing of our spirit. Only Jesus is the bread that never fails. In him, we will never hunger or thirst again.

The greatest spiritual gift is not what God gives us, but who He is. Jesus gave the people bread, then he became their bread. The people who ate the bread Jesus gave them were satisfied for a day, but those who received Jesus as their bread were satisfied for eternity. We cannot be so focused on what God gives us that we miss who He is. God is our bread. God is our provision. In Him, we have everything we will ever need. In Him, our spiritual hunger will be satisfied. In Him, our deepest longings will be filled, and our searching will end.

Prayer for Today

FATHER GOD,

You are my provision. In You, I have everything I will ever need. My body may hunger, but my spirit is full. You have given me eternity in Your presence. My spirit will never hunger or thirst again because Jesus is the bread of life. I receive Your gifts, I receive Your blessings, and I turn to You, the Giver of all things. There is nothing I want more than You.

Amen

"I am the true vine."
John 15:5

When I was about three years old, my mother was a florist. I often watched her carefully prune and trim plants she was nursing back to health. One day, I wanted to be helpful so I took a pair of scissors to one of her plants. In my clumsy attempt to prune the plant, I destroyed it. I cut every branch, leaf, and twig off the poor thing. Every leaf I severed from the plant died.

Jesus tells us that he is the vine, and we are the branches. The vine is the root that feeds, nourishes, and sustains the branches. Every branch that isn't connected to the vine will wither and die. We may bud and flower, we may look pretty and full of life, but that doesn't come from us. We are sustained by Jesus, the true vine. Our work, our looks, our houses, our cars, our education, none of that will give us life, none of that will keep us strong and vibrant. It is only by staying attached to the vine that we flourish.

In a culture that esteems independence and self-sufficiency, it isn't popular to say that we are dependent, but we are. We are dependent on God. He is the source of our strength. He is the source of our life. Many people turn to other sources of life hoping to find fulfillment. Some turn to drugs or alcohol, some to work or success. Others turn to relationships, shopping, or fame, but none of that will sustain for long. True life comes from being attached to the true vine.

It can be easy to get so busy with doing things for God, that we forget to stay close to Him. We run from place to place doing good things. We spend time and energy serving, but we neglect the nourishment that comes from being connected to Jesus. Every day we must be close to our vine, receiving from him, being nourished by him in order to be effective in our service for him. God is more concerned about our relationship *with* Him than He is about our service *for* Him. It is in our relationship that we grow. He reveals Himself more to us, He teaches us, and guides us when we invest time in being close to Him. We must be as close to God as a branch is to the vine. The further we wander from God, the more we wither.

Jesus calls us to remain in him. "Remain in me, as I also remain in you. No branch can bear fruit by itself; it must remain in the vine. Neither can you bear fruit unless you remain in me" (John 15:4). God wants us to remain in Him. We don't stop by for a quick fill up and then go off on our own again. God calls us to remain in His presence, that is where our strength comes from. Remain in God's presence, and you will flourish.

Prayer for Today

FATHER GOD,

My strength comes from You. In You I have abundant life. Teach me how to remain in Your presence. I want to be as close to You as a branch is to a vine. Let my life be filled with Your presence, let me flourish because I belong to You, and let others see Your life and Your love at work in me.

Amen

"I am the way, the truth, and the life."
John 14:6

When my husband was an active duty Marine, we moved several times. On the final segment of our final move across the country, we had two vehicles. My husband drove in front, and I followed him. At one point, he unexpectedly exited the freeway. I was confused. This wasn't the way. We still had a hundred miles to go. I followed him, worry and uncertainty growing in my mind. He pulled over in a small parking lot, and I parked beside him. When I asked him why we stopped, he smiled and pointed at the beach. Our children squealed with joy and ran to the water. It was the first time they had seen the Pacific Ocean.

During the Last Supper, as Jesus prepared to walk to the cross, knowing what was awaiting him, Jesus told his disciples that he was going away to prepare a place for them. He said, "You know the way to the place where I am going" (John 14:4). The disciples were confused. They heard Jesus say he was leaving, and they didn't know where he was going. Though Jesus said they knew the way, they couldn't be sure. "Thomas said to him, 'Lord, we don't know where you are going, so how can we know the way?'" (John 14:5).

Jesus replied, "I am the way and the truth and the life" (John 14:6).

The disciples already knew the way because they knew Jesus. Jesus is the way. Following him is the only map we need. On our trip, my husband turned off of our planned route. He changed directions, and I followed him to something much better than I had planned. We may try to plan out our lives, charting our course, diligently mapping out our path, but Jesus is the only way. He is the one we need to follow. We don't have to find the way ourselves because we know Jesus, and he is the way.

Life doesn't always go the way we plan. Detours happen. Routes change. Obstacles end up in our path. No matter how carefully we plan, sometimes the road in front of us shifts. Our journey may change, but the way doesn't. Jesus is the way that always points us home. We may not always know the road we're walking, but we know who is leading us. If we follow him we will always arrive at our destination.

Prayer for Today

LORD GOD,

You are the way. I will follow You. You make a way where there is no way. You made a path through the sea, and a way in the wilderness. You are always leading me according to Your perfect will. Help me to follow You no matter where You lead. I may not know the map, but I know You, and that is all I need.

Amen

"I am the Lord your God who brought you out of Egypt, out of
the land of slavery."
Deuteronomy 5:6

The Israelites were in bondage in Egypt. The work of Joseph had been forgotten. The rulers of Egypt had turned against the Israelites. For four hundred years, they were enslaved. They labored for the Egyptians, and their children were murdered. Then they cried out to God, and He heard them. He sent Moses to free them and lead them into the land He had promised to Abraham, Isaac, and Jacob. The Israelites could not free themselves, it was God who rescued them.

God is still rescuing people. We were trapped in bondage, enslaved by sin until God sent Jesus to be our rescue. The cross set us free. We were led from a land of slavery into a land of grace. Just as God freed the Israelites and led them through the wilderness, God is leading us. He did not set the Israelites free and then abandon them. God was their guide, and He led them every step of the way. He led them into their inheritance, into the land He had prepared for them. God is our light in the darkness. When we follow Him, He leads us into something greater, something better than anything we've had before.

Sometimes the journey takes longer than we'd like. Because of their disobedience, it took the Israelites took forty years in the wilderness to make a three-day trip. We might want God to instantly transport us to the Promised Land, but it is the journey through the wilderness that makes us ready for the Promised Land. We might not yet have arrived at our destination, but thanks to the grace of God we're no longer where we started.

God hears the cries of His people. He hears when we pray for deliverance, help, and rescue. God is our redemption. God is the One who breaks the bondage of sin and shame. He is the One who overcomes death itself to set His people free. There is no chain so strong that God cannot break it. There is no addiction, fear, habit, sin, or mistake so powerful that God cannot redeem. He has already won the battle. He is your Redeemer. Your freedom has been won, and it cannot be taken from you.

Prayer for Today

MIGHTY GOD,

You are my rescuer. When circumstances try to overwhelm me, when life feels too hard, I turn to You, Lord. You have won my freedom. You have freed me from the bondage of sin. You have severed the chains that held me down. I will follow You through the wilderness. I will follow You until You bring me into the Promised Land. Thank you for hearing my cry and rescuing me.

Amen

DAY TWENTY-TWO

GOD IS LOVE

"I am slow to anger and filled with unfailing love and
faithfulness."
Exodus 34:6 (NLT)

When Moses asked to see God, God hid him in the cleft of a rock and covered him with His hand as he passed by. He shielded Moses from seeing His face, letting Moses see only His back. In His mercy, He protected Moses from what his eyes could not see. As He passed by, God proclaimed this about Himself, "I am slow to anger and filled with unfailing love and faithfulness" (Exodus 34:6, NLT). Of all the things He could have declared about His character in that moment, God chose His patience, His love, and His faithfulness.

Too many people have the idea of God as a disapproving Father waiting to punish them when they mess up. They spend too many years worried that God is mad at them, assuming that He is disappointed in them. Instead of turning to God, they hide from Him.

But God tells us that He is loving, slow to anger, and full of compassion. God isn't sitting on His throne waiting to squash us if we make a mistake. He is waiting to pick us up when we fall. God's love is unfailing. It's not just that His love won't fail; His love for us is incapable of failing. No power in Heaven or on Earth can overcome His love. In His own words, God tells us, "I have loved you with an everlasting love" (Jeremiah 31:3). His love for you is unfailing and everlasting. It cannot fail, and it cannot end.

Because of His great love, He is slow to anger. We may fail time and time again, but God never does. We may go the wrong way, we may make a mistake, we may even make a huge mistake, but God's love is still there. He is patient with us, calling us home, and drawing us to Him even when we run the other way. God has opened the way to salvation for us because He doesn't want anyone to perish. His is slow to anger and full of mercy because He is our loving Father, and He wants His children to come home.

We may falter in our faith, we may run from God, but He is faithful. He never gives up on us. God does not change His mind. He does not love us one day and cast us away the next. God's love is forever. His faithfulness will never end. He never breaks a promise, and He never goes back on His word. God will never betray you. Faithfulness is a part of who He is. No matter what comes our way, we can live in peace because we know God's love is unending, and His faithfulness always endures.

Prayer for Today

MIGHTY GOD,

You are a loving and patient Father. You are the Faithful One. You will never leave me, and You will never betray me. I trust You, Lord, because You never fail. Help me to remember that You are not waiting for me to make a mistake, but that You long to bless me. You will be by my side now and forever. Your love and Your faithfulness will never end.

Amen

GOD IS ALWAYS THE SAME

"I am the Lord and I do not change."
Malachi 3:6

When I was in elementary school, I had a friend who changed her mind constantly. One day I was her best friend, the next day she didn't like me. Back and forth she went. I never knew where I stood with her. Would she play with me at recess, or wouldn't she? The uncertainty was awful. I was held captive by her changing moods, and there was no security in our friendship.

Too many people think God takes that same unpredictable approach to us. He loves us when we're good, and He's mad at us when we're bad. They struggle to trust God because they think He must be like us, subject to changing emotions and shifting allegiances. Because they have been hurt, abandoned, or treated unfairly by people they once trusted, they approach God with hesitation, expecting Him to change His mind. They wait in nervous anticipation for God to figure out who they really are and change His mind about loving them.

But that is not God.

God is unchanging. He is the same yesterday, today, and forever (Hebrews 13:8). God is perfect, therefore He cannot change. He is not learning, evolving, or improving. God is God. He is the same God now that He was at the dawn of creation. He is the same God who saw His Son suffer on the cross. He is the same God today as He will be at the end of time. The universe itself might change, but God does not.

Because God does not change, His Word is always true. His plan for redemption still stands, and His promises will never fail. We can trust what God says because His Word does not change. God says that you are loved, and you are. That cannot change because the One who spoke those words does not change. God is not like us. He is not subject to emotional swings or shifting moods. He will not change His mind because He suddenly learns something new about you. God already knows everything about you, and His love for you is unchanging.

We may change, but God does not. We may make a mistake, we may miss a step, but none of that changes His love. God's love for us is not dependent on what we do, it is dependent on who He is. You can trust that God's promises are true now and always. He will not love you one day and reject you the next. You can be secure, safe, and at peace in His promises because God never changes.

Prayer for Today

LORD GOD,

Thank you for Your faithfulness. You are the same today as You were at the beginning of creation. I trust Your Word is true. I trust Your promises will never be broken. I believe that Your love for me is unchanging. You are not a God who changes His mind. I can be secure in Your loving arms because I know that You will never leave me or forsake me. I am Yours today and always.

Amen

"I am your shield."
Genesis 15:1

When my husband was in the Marine Corps, he deployed to combat three times. Three times I watched him pack up his gear and go to war. In addition to socks, uniforms, and boots, he also had his helmet, his weapon, and his Kevlar vest. I tried on his vest once, and I almost fell over. It was heavy and thick, a layer of metal that would help protect him from enemy fire. In the battles he would face, that vest was his physical shield.

Many of us will never go to war, but we will all face spiritual battles. In those battles, God is our shield. Throughout history, soldiers have carried shields into battle. The shield is a protection and a shelter. In Genesis 15:1, God speaks to Abraham and tells him, "Do not be afraid, Abram, I am your shield, your very great reward." God spoke these words right before He made a covenant with Abraham. God promised him that the land of Canaan would belong to him and his descendants. He was calling Abraham into a new land and into a new destiny. God was leading Abraham to a place he had never been, and His promise was that He Himself would be Abraham's shield. Abraham didn't need to fear because God would be his protection.

When we carry a shield, we carry it in front of our body. The shield goes first. God is our shield, and He goes before us. God stands before us as our defense and our protection. He is our shelter and our covering. Anything the enemy fires at us must first go through the shield of God, and His shield never fails. A shield doesn't do much good if we step outside of its protection. When we hide ourselves in God's protection, His shield is our unfailing defense and shelter. Jesus Christ showed us the power of the shield of faith when he went to the cross. Jesus was the shield between us and the wrath of God.

Ephesians 6 gives us a powerful depiction of the armor of God. One of the pieces of armor we are called to carry is the shield of faith. Our shield comes from our faith in God. It is faith that protects us from the attacks of the enemy. It isn't the works we do, how many hours we read the Bible, or how long we pray. Faith is our defense. Our faith in God's plan, His power, His mercy, and His grace is our defense. When we rely on God and trust in Him, we cannot be defeated by lies of the enemy or circumstances that threaten us because our faith is our shield. We may be in terrible trials or situations that seem impossible, but when we hold on to our faith, our shield is intact. God is our protection and our shelter in the midst of every storm.

Prayer for Today

MIGHTY GOD,

Lord, You are my shield and my protection. I hide myself in the shelter of Your love and grace. You are my covering, and You will not fail. Nothing can overcome Your protection. I will not fear because You are my shield. I carry the shield of faith, emblazoned with the cross of Jesus Christ. I belong to You and You will be my protection.

Amen

DAY TWENTY-FIVE

GOD IS CALLING YOU

"I am the Lord, the God of Israel, who summons you by name."
Isaiah 45:3

God knows your name. He sees you, He hears you, and He summons you. From before time began, you have been a part of His plan. You are not an after-thought, you are not an accident, and you are not a product of luck and happenstance. You were intentionally and lovingly created by God Almighty. You are here at this time and in this place because He has summoned you by name.

You may feel overlooked, unappreciated, and invisible, but that is not who you are. You are called, chosen, and anointed for such a time as this. God is summoning you. He calls your name because He has work for you to do. God is all-powerful, all-knowing, and completely self-sufficient. He doesn't need us, He chooses us. God has chosen you to be a part of His plan for this world. Every day you have a choice to accept or reject the work He has called you to do. You can listen to His voice and follow

His leading, or you can close your heart to it and go your own way. The choice is always yours.

In the Old Testament, a young Jewish woman named Esther unexpectedly becomes Queen of Persia. In the midst of her life of royalty and comfort, she is called to a dangerous and terrifying task. The Jewish people are being threatened with annihilation. She is the only one who can go to the king and plead for their lives, but to approach the king without being summoned is to risk death. Esther is scared, but her uncle tells her, "Do not think that because you are in the king's house you alone of all the Jews will escape. For if you remain silent at this time, relief and deliverance for the Jews will arise from another place, but you and your father's family will perish. And who knows but that you have come to your royal position for such a time as this?" (Esther 4:13-14). Esther is not just being asked to help her people, she is being given the chance to be a part of God's plan for redemption. God didn't need Esther to save His people. He was choosing her to be a part of His plan. She was called, summoned not by an earthly king, but by God Himself to take her place in His plan.

God is calling you. Your life has purpose. You were created for a reason. You are here for such a time as this, to stand, to risk, and to serve. God has chosen you.

Prayer for Today

Mighty God,

I believe You have called me. I am not an accident. I am part of Your plan and Your design. Speak, Lord, and I will listen. Lead, Lord, and I will go. Strengthen me to stand firm in faith, to believe in You when the world tells me to doubt, and to trust You even when it's hard. Here I am, Lord, send me.

Amen

GOD IS YOUR TEACHER

"I am the Lord, your God, who teaches you what is best, who directs you in the way you should go."
Isaiah 48:17

*D*o you remember pop quizzes in school? Sitting at your desk, thinking everything was fine and then BAM! Pop quiz. A sudden, unexpected test. Did you know enough? Were you prepared? Had you been paying attention? In one moment, everything you knew was going to be put to the test, and you would pass or fail all on your own. Fortunately for us, God doesn't operate like that. God is not hiding the answers. He isn't sitting behind a desk ready to fail you if you get a question wrong. In fact, if you ask, God will give you the answers you need.

After the Israelites left Egypt, God went before them as a pillar of cloud by day and a pillar of fire by night. When the cloud rose, the Israelites knew it was time to move. Throughout the dark hours of the night, the fire of God's presence was with them. They never had to choose which way to go, or what to do next because God was leading them. He was the answer they needed.

God is still leading us today. His presence is with us. We have not been left to wander and find our own way. God is not making it hard for you. He isn't trying to trick you. He is willing to show you the direction you need to go. He is willing to give you everything you need to accomplish His plan and His purpose for your life. God has not set you up for failure, instead He has given you everything you need to succeed. It is all available to you if you are willing to ask. "Ask and it will be given to you; seek and you will find; knock and the door will be opened to you" (Matthew 7:7). The question isn't whether you know all the answers, the question is do you know the One who has the answers?

Your life is a precious gift from God. His hand is open to you. His voice is leading you. He holds everything you need, and He is willing to give it to you. Life is not a pop quiz, it's an open-book test. Turn to His Word and hear His voice. Open His book and you will find answers. The Bible still speaks. God's Word is unchanging, and it is powerful. It is as true today as it was the day it was written. Read His Word and speak it out loud, hear what God is saying to you, and you will find the answers you need. God has not left you on your own. He is not waiting for you to fail. He has given you His Word, and He is with you.

Prayer for Today

FATHER GOD,

Thank you, Lord, for never leaving me. You have given me Your

Word to teach me and Your Holy Spirit to guide me. You are not hiding from me. You are always with me. I turn to You because You have the answers to all of my questions. I seek You, Lord, and trust that You are all I need.

Amen

"I am doing a new thing."
Isaiah 43:19

The first time I spoke in a women's prison, I was terrified. I had never been to a prison before much less a maximum-security prison where I would be speaking only a short distance away from death row. I had never done anything like it. The metal detectors, the identification check, the armed guards that walked me to the chapel, it was all unfamiliar territory. I was in a new land, and I had no choice but to walk where God led.

God is constantly doing new things. While we are tempted to rely on what we know, cling to the familiar and wait for things to be the way they've always been, God is ready to do something new. He may be doing a new thing in your life right this moment. No matter how much we have done or how far we have come, we will never be done. God has new land for us, new ministry, new influence, new gifts to be revealed, new talents to be used. God is always ready to do more, give more, and supply more. His love will never run out, and His calling will never stop. God will always have more for you. You are never past your prime with God. "Forget the former things; do not dwell on the past. See, I am doing a new thing! Now it springs up; do you not perceive it? I am making a way in the wilderness and streams in the wasteland" (Isaiah 43:18-19).

We cannot see the new thing God is doing, and we cannot move into new land if we cling to the past. We cannot hold on to our past victories or our defeats. Looking backward will not help when we are called to move forward. The Apostle Paul knew this. He had both great victories and terrible defeats in his past. He was a man who persecuted, arrested, and killed Christians before he had a life-changing meeting with Jesus. Paul's past was terrible and bitter, but he moved forward, spreading the Gospel of Jesus Christ. "But one thing I do: Forgetting what is behind and straining toward what is ahead, I press on toward the goal to win the prize for which God has called me heavenward in Christ Jesus" (Philippians 3:13-14). Paul didn't dwell on his past mistakes, and he didn't rest on his past victories. He kept pressing on, moving forward in his mission.

You may have great accomplishments in your past, or there may be terrible failures lying there. Whatever is in your past, God is not done with you. Your work is not done. God is calling you to forget the former things because He is doing something new. God is at work, and He isn't done with you.

Prayer for Today

MIGHTY GOD,

Thank You for not being done with me. My best days are not behind me. You are doing a new thing in my life. Give me eyes to see Your hand at work. I am ready for something new. I will stop looking at the things in my past and keep my focus on You. I will wait in joyful expectation for what You are going to do.

Amen

DAY TWENTY-EIGHT

GOD IS YOUR HOPE

"I am the resurrection and the life."
John 11:25

In the Gospel of John, we read the story of a man named Lazarus who died. When Jesus comes to the town of Bethany and sees Lazarus's sister, Martha, he tells her that Lazarus will rise again. "Martha answered, 'I know he will rise at the resurrection at the last day'" (John 11:24). In her grief, Martha professes her belief in eternal life. She knows that she will see her brother again. She believes in the resurrection to come. But then Jesus speaks, and changes everything. "I am the resurrection and the life" (John 11:25). The resurrection isn't a far-off event. The resurrection is a person.

Jesus Christ is the resurrection. Eternal life is in him. Jesus has broken the power of death. Martha was looking forward to an event that would come at the last day, but Jesus says that event is now. He calls Lazarus out of the tomb. He speaks, and death is defeated. Not even death can stand against the power of God.

Jesus laid down his life, and three days later took it up again. God speaks, and life flows from His words. He is the Living One.

Lazarus was dead, and yet God restored and redeemed him. There is nothing so hopeless that God cannot turn it for good. Jesus called Lazarus out of the darkness of the grave and restored him to life. What seemed like the end for Lazarus, was only the beginning. God can take all of the broken pieces of our lives and breathe life into them again. God can take the dead areas of our lives and resurrect them. Relationships that have been broken, finances that have been ruined, lives that have fallen into despair and depravity, God can call into those graves and bring life out of them.

Death itself must answer to God. There is nothing in your life that is beyond His redemption. There is no secret in your past, no mistake you've made, no regret or disappointment, that God cannot call from the shadows and bring into His light. Every step you've taken can become a testimony of His resurrection power if you place it in His hands. Jesus told them to roll away the stone that covered Lazarus's grave. "Jesus called out in a loud voice, 'Lazarus, come out!' The dead man came out, his hands and feet wrapped with strips of linen, and a cloth around his face. Jesus said to them, 'Take off the grave clothes and let him go'" (John 11:43-44).

Jesus has called you out of death and into life. The grave clothes that bound you no longer belong to you. Names you were called, whispers that were spoken about you, none of that belongs to you anymore. Jesus is the resurrection, and he has called your name. The grave clothes of your past have been loosed, and you have been given new life.

Prayer for Today

Mighty God,

You are the God of life. Not even death can stand against You. You have redeemed me. You called my name, and I walked out of the grave and into the eternal life You have given me. The chains of my past do not hold me anymore. I have been set free by Your amazing grace. Today and every day, I live for You.

Amen

"I am coming soon."
Revelation 22:20

When my children were younger, the weeks leading up to Christmas were filled with excitement and anticipation. Every day they asked if it was Christmas. Is today Christmas? Is it Christmas yet? Soon, we would reply. Christmas was coming soon, but soon was never soon enough for them. Then, finally, they woke up on Christmas morning, and all the waiting was worth it.

In Revelation 22:20, Jesus says that he is returning soon. But how soon, we ask. What is soon? Is it today? Is he coming now? As believers we have that same anticipation, that same excited longing, knowing something wonderful is coming but not knowing when. When is he coming? The truth is, we don't know. It could be today, it could a hundred years from now. We don't know the timing, only God does, but we know the promise. He is coming. Our task is to live in expectant awareness. Our Lord is returning soon, so we must be ready.

The Greek word used here for soon is *tachu* and it means without delay, or suddenly. There is no delay to God's return. He is not being held back or restrained. This is God's plan unfolding according to His timing. We wait in expectation for Jesus to return, and his return will be *tachu,* suddenly he will return. He will return with the armies of Heaven with him. Victory will be with him as he triumphs over every adversary. Like lightening that is seen across the sky, Jesus our King will return. We're not going to get advance notice, there won't be a movie trailer to prepare us for opening day. Suddenly, Jesus will return.

This is our hope. Jesus is coming soon. We're almost home. We have not been forgotten; we have not been abandoned. Chaos may rise around us, and times may be hard, but our hope is in the King of Kings and the Lord of Lords. God keeps His promises. Jesus promised to return, and he will. "The Lord is not slow in keeping his promise, as some understand slowness. Instead he is patient with you, not wanting anyone to perish, but everyone to come to repentance" (2 Peter 3:9). God is not slow; He is patient. He is not hesitating; He is calling. God is giving each of us every opportunity to hear His voice and be ready for His return. The same waiting that makes believers ask "Where is he?" is the same waiting that is calling unbelievers home.

It is in this waiting that we are called to proclaim His grace. God wants every one of His children to turn to Him, to confess the name of Jesus and be saved, but time is short. He is coming soon. This time, right now, is the only chance we have to share the Good News of the cross. We won't be sharing the Gospel in Heaven, everyone there already knows it. God's plan for eternity is unfolding, and He has called you to be a part of it. This is your chance. Keep your eyes on the promise and be ready. Jesus is coming soon.

Prayer for Today

MIGHTY GOD,

You are my God, my Savior, and my Comforter. You are the Author and Finisher of my faith. You are the first and the last, the beginning and the end. Your promise is sure. Help me to share the Gospel with those who don't know You. Time is short, and You are coming soon to bring us to eternity in Your presence. Come quickly, Lord Jesus!

Amen

GOD IS VICTORIOUS

"I am the Living One."
Revelation 1:18

When Jesus went to the cross, beaten and tortured, it must have looked like a defeat. The man who said he was the Son of God was nailed to a cross to suffer and die. The one who had healed others, raised people from the dead, and multiplied food to feed thousands, was crucified. While he was hanging on a cross, naked and humiliated, his followers fled. It was a day of darkness and sorrow. He was laid in a tomb, and a stone rolled in front of the entrance. Jesus was dead.

Three days later, he rose again. He walked out of the tomb in victory. His death shattered the chains of sin and broke the hold of death itself. Jesus is alive. "I am the Living One; I was dead, and now look, I am alive for ever and ever! And I hold the keys of death and Hades" (Revelation 1:18). Jesus Christ is alive forevermore. His death was not a defeat but a triumph. He is seated in

Heaven, and he holds the keys to death and Hades. We do not have to fear death or Hell because Jesus is the one who holds the keys, and since we belong to him, death has no claim on us.

God is victorious. He has trampled sin and death. He has redeemed and restored those who were lost in sin. He made a way to eternity. He paid a debt that was too great for us to bear. He gave us his righteousness so we can stand before God without fear of condemnation or rejection. Through the blood of Jesus, we can walk in victory.

Our God is undefeated. He is the One who fights our battles. He is the Living One, and He reigns forever and ever. We can live free from fear because we belong to the One who cannot be shaken. God has not given you a spirit of fear, but a life of victory. You belong to God Almighty, and nothing can snatch you from His hand. No mistake you make, no failure, no abuse that you suffer, no time you stumble, no disappointment or regret can change the victory that Jesus Christ has already won.

God chose you before the foundation of the world. He has called you by name. He has prepared a place for you. Your eternity is secure. Your destiny is to live in the presence of God. Rejoice in God. Praise His name because you belong to Him! Lift up your head, and shout for joy! One day you will stand before the Living One, see the scars that bought your freedom, and hear the voice that commands the winds say, "Well done."

Prayer for Today

EVERLASTING GOD,

You are the Living One. You are victorious. You have conquered sin and death, and You live forevermore. You are undefeated. Nothing can overcome You. My future is secure because I belong to You. I will live in joyful expectation knowing my life is in Your hands. Bless me, Lord. Strengthen me, Lord. Lead me, Lord. You are my God, and You have already won the victory!

Amen

You Are...Thirty Names God Has Given You and What They Mean

God knows you. He knows your hopes and your dreams, your deepest secrets and your greatest wounds. He knows who you are, and He has called you by name.

Take a thirty day devotional journey to learn about the names God has given you, what they mean, and how they can change your life.

Mission Hollywood

A Hollywood bad boy. A pastor's daughter. What could possibly go wrong?

Rocked by sandal, his career in jeopardy, movie star Ben Prescott agrees to volunteer at a small Hollywood church. When he meets Lily Shaw, Ben must risk his career to follow his heart, but Lily wants the one thing he doesn't have: faith

Made in Hollywood

When a pastor's son saves her life, a prodigal daughter dares to believe in second chances.

Hannah left her family and her faith when she ran away to Hollywood. Abandoned and alone, she's lost hope, until the night Noah Shaw saves her life. When the shadows of her former life threaten to expose her past, she must chose between running or fighting for the new life she's built and the man she's grown to love.

Michelle is a wife, homeschooling mom, and multi-genre author. When she isn't writing, she is reading, hiking, or baking something involving chocolate.

Michelle loves to hear from readers. You can connect with her on Twitter, Facebook, or Instagram @MKeenerWrites.

If you are interested in joining a launch team for one of her new books or scheduling Michelle as a speaker check out her website www.MichelleKeener.com

For information on bulk order discounts of *You Are...* or *I Am...* for your church, please email info@MichelleKeener.com

www.ingramcontent.com/pod-product-compliance
Lightning Source LLC
Chambersburg PA
CBHW051004050726
47592CB00007B/2702